TURNING POINT

FROM ASHES
TO BEAUTY

TURNING POINT

FROM ASHES TO BEAUTY

TASSHA FAISON

**TURNING POINT:
FROM ASHES TO BEAUTY**

Copyright © 2016 Tassha Faison

All rights reserved. This book is protected by the copyright laws of the United States of America and should not be copied or reprinted for commercial gain or profit. The use of short quotations or occasional page copying for personal or group study is permitted and encouraged upon request. Unless otherwise identified, Scripture quotations are from the Holy Bible, King James Version. All emphasis within quoted Scripture is the author's own.

ISBN: 978-1-945456-68-8

Cover Design:
Yakisha Comer - COMPEL ONE

Editor:
Rekesha Pittman

Turning Point Life Coaching, LLC
PO Box 627 - Alma, GA 31510.

Email: tasshafaison@gmail.com
Tel: 401-542-TURN

TABLE OF CONTENTS

Dedication
Foreword
Acknowledgements
Introduction

CHAPTER 1
A TURNING POINT IS POSSIBLE   1

CHAPTER 2
ABRAHAM'S TURNING POINT!   5

CHAPTER 3
JOSEPH'S TURNING POINT!   13

CHAPTER 4
MOSES' TURNING POINT!   21

CHAPTER 5
GIDEON'S TURNING POINT!   27

CHAPTER 6
NICODEMUS' TURNING POINT!   33

CHAPTER 7
THE WOMAN AT THE WELL   37

CHAPTER 8
THE ADULTEROUS WOMAN   43

CHAPTER 9
THE TWELVE APOSTLES   49

CHAPTER 10
PAUL'S TURNING POINT!   57

CHAPTER 11
MY STORY & MY TURNING POINT!   63

CHAPTER 12
REFLECTION SCRIPTURES AND HELPFUL QUOTES   67

DEDICATION

To my dad, Lester Brown.

Turning Point is dedicated to those who are at their wit's end.

This inspirational and motivational manual is to encourage and help with building your faith in God for a turnaround from ashes to beauty and from a setback to a setup for a comeback.

Minister Tassha Faison being ordained into the Apostolic Prophetic Ministry by Apostle Elizabeth Hairston-McBurrows

FOREWORD

Turning is a significant action in the Bible because it is something that we must choose to do. Throughout this book, Minister Tassha Faison provides key examples of flawed people who decided to turn and follow God. She encourages all of us who are imperfect to embrace the One who is for true redemption.

Turning Point will encourage those who may see ashes now, but will soon witness beauty on the horizon. Her encouragement, passion and straight talk approach invites the reader to discover how he or she can reach a personal turning point. This is a book for someone who needs real solutions.

Prepare to delve in to a few stories that will parallel similar instances in your own life. Just like the people presented here, you can turn and find a way of escape that will bless your life. If you are ready for a change, turn these pages and get right to the point.

Rekesha Pittman,
Get Write Publishing

ACKNOWLEDGEMENTS

I would like to express my gratitude to Dr. Benard Etta, who said to me, "Just write," and the rest will come. I am so thankful for His Godly wisdom and support in the editing and publishing of this book.

I also give thanks to the many people who saw me through this book; to all those who provided support, talked things over, read, wrote, offered comments, allowed me to quote their remarks and assisted in the editing, proofreading, and design.

Above all, I give honor to God, who gave me the courage to begin this journey of a thousand miles with this first step.

I would like to thank and express my love to my two young sons, D'Angelo and Dillon; you are truly my inspiration. Thanks for keeping me on my toes at all times.

I want to thanks James Cobb for being a support to me and my boys during our journey. We appreciate you!

I thought this journey would be long and challenging, but the inspiration I received from the leaders and mentors God placed on my path, instead made the experience exciting.

I would also like to thank my Spiritual Mother, Apostle Elizabeth Hairston-McBurrows, for her constant outpouring of love and wisdom from her heart and from above into me.

Much love to Dr. Larry Phillip Brown for covering me in his prayers and leadership as I continue the journey God has set before me.

I also would like to thank my mother, Laura Waites for always believing in me.

To my friends Kimberly Hamm, Tawanna Bailey, Apostle Janet Clary, Joseph Holley, Tara Shuman, my aunt Cassandra Miller, Elizabeth West, Caroline Lott and Elder Marcus Hill, thank you for being the ears that listened and the shoulders I was able to lean on.

Last but not least, I beg forgiveness of all those who have been with me over the course of the years, whose names I have failed to mention. May the good Lord bless you all!

Special thanks and love to Dillon Gooding, Sr. for everything. Our sons are who they are because of you. R.I.P. 10-20-1967 to 07-28-2016

INTRODUCTION

There are more people in the world today than at any other time in the history of the human race, who are not happy with the state of their lives. Some of them are where they are as a result of the choices they made, while others, as a consequence of the choices made by others on their behalf which affected them. Most people today are depressed by the thought of where they have ended up. Others, are angered, while some are confused. Reactions vary depending on individual situations and circumstances.

Are you one of the people mentioned above? Does the thought of where you are in your life at the moment "cause pain in your chest?" Do you find yourself questioning how you ended up where you are, and where you are headed?

Maybe you have been crying out to God trying to figure out what on earth has been going on. Perhaps you are tired of complaining about the same things, and all you want to see is a change. Some of you might be past the point of waiting for a change. Maybe you have given up.

I would like to tell you, don't give up. It is time to find your hope again. "There is hope for a living dog than a dead lion." As long as you are still breathing, you aren't supposed to give up or lose hope.

Where you are right now is not permanent, it doesn't have to be. This does not have to be how the rest of your life goes. It is not too late for something to change. Your life is the perfect candidate for a turning point.

A turning point can be defined as a moment a significant change occurs in the life of an individual, leading to a better outcome. A turning point is when everything changes for the better, from ashes to beauty. A turning point is the defining moment many people remember when their lives changed.

It is worth noting that you cannot do it alone. God is there to guide you and help you through the process of change. God's desire for your life is for you to be above your circumstances. He wants to see you working efficiently, bringing glory to His name. He wishes to see you fulfill what He has assigned you to do.

With God, know that nothing is impossible
- Luke 1:37

There is nothing He cannot do. There is no point in a person's life that God will say, "I cannot do this," or "I am done." God has provided you with the grace you need to be able to experience a total turnaround in your life. As weak as you may be right now, your weakness does not discourage God. His grace abounds in your weakness.

"But he said to me, "My grace is sufficient for you, for my power is made perfect in weakness." Therefore I will boast all the more gladly about my weaknesses, so that Christ's power may rest on me."

- 2 Corinthians 12:9 (ESV)

This book will take you through many biblical examples of people who experienced a turning point in their lives. This book is here to tell you that it is not too late. You do not have to settle for your present circumstances. Your life is not meant to be a life filled with disappointment, failure, and misdirection. God has called you for a particular purpose, and He will see you through it.

This book is here to help you find hope again. It is here, hopefully, to teach you something. It is also here to show you that you are not alone in what you are going through and your current situation does not have to last forever. This book is here to encourage you and help you find the strength to get up and take steps in a new direction.

Remember that where you are is not permanent. No matter what you have gone through, everything can and will work out for your good. As you read this book, carry these words in your mind. As you see more and more accounts of those who also had a defining moment in their lives—a turning point—know that the same thing can and will happen for you.

"And we know that all things work together for good to those who love God, to those who are the called according to His purpose."

- Romans 8:28 (NKJV)

Chapter 1

A TURNING POINT IS POSSIBLE

God can make something good out of nothing, but our cooperation is needed.

The Bible has countless accounts of people whose lives experienced a turnaround completely and God was involved in it all. That is what happens when we come in contact with the Father, realizing that He has all it takes to bring a new direction in our lives, despite what we are facing.

A setback in life is not the end, but it can become a setup for a comeback. Problems can turn into opportunities through the grace of God. God can turn our mess into a message and our trash into treasure if we choose to give it to Him. As great as God is, He can't force Himself into our lives. We have to come to Him in faith and willingly hand the broken pieces of our lives to Him. God can make something good out of nothing, but our cooperation is needed.

TURNING POINT: FROM ASHES TO BEAUTY

Then I went down to the potter's house, and, behold, he wrought a work on the wheels. And the vessel that he made of clay was marred in the hand of the potter: so he made it again another vessel, as seemed good to the potter to make it.

- Jeremiah 18:3-4

As seen in the above biblical text, even though the vessel made of clay became marred in the hand of the potter, the potter made it again into another vessel, better than what it was before. That is what God does with everyone who yields themselves to him. A turnaround is possible, but a turning point cannot happen in our lives without us doing our part. We have to be on the same page with God. Our willingness to move and act in faith is crucial to experiencing a turning point.

As recorded in several Biblical accounts, many people encountered God in both the Old and New Testament, but only a few experienced change. Why? They were the ones who cooperated with God. God can't force Himself nor impose His will on us; He needs our agreement. Every person who encountered a change in their life, took a step of faith in one way or another. We can see this from Abraham to the Twelve disciples and many others in the Bible. They encountered God in one way or another, and their lives were never the same.

Look at someone like Joseph, in the Old Testament. His life was not the best for a while, but he never stopped. He never gave up. He never settled for his circumstances. He was hated by his brothers, pitted, potted, sold as a slave, accused and imprisoned, but God brought him to a turning point as written in these scriptures.

He sent a man before them, even Joseph, who was sold for a servant: Whose feet they hurt with fetters: he was laid in iron: Until the time that his word came: the word of the LORD tried him. The king sent and loosed him; even the ruler of the people, and let him go free. He made him lord of his house, and ruler of all his substance: To bind his princes at his pleasure; and teach his senators wisdom.

- Psalm 105:17-22

If God took Joseph from prison to the palace, He can do the same for you. God can bring a turning point to your life.

TURNING POINT: FROM ASHES TO BEAUTY

God can shift you from shame and give you a name! He can turn your ashes into beauty and your mourning into dancing. (Psalm 30:11). That is God for you! If he did it for Joseph, He will do it for you if you dare to believe and refuse to give up.

All those who experienced a turning point in scriptures had different encounters. Although their turning points were in various ways, the same result came through for all of them—their lives were never the same. Their lives changed for the better and the best. You are the next in the line for a miracle.

Chapter 2

ABRAHAM'S TURNING POINT

Do not sit complacently when things are not going the right way. Avoid complaining – your words can be used for much more productive and powerful things.

Abraham is known for having great faith. Paul speaks of Abraham's faith in Romans 4 and Hebrews 11. Many people refer to Abraham when they talk about faith. They talk of the prosperous life he lived as a result of his obedience to God. They speak of the miracle that he and his wife Sarah experienced at an old age. Having a child was a turning point in their lives.

Abraham came to the spotlight in Scripture the day the Lord told him to leave his father's house and he obeyed (Gen 12:1). Before that time, there was nothing extraordinary about Abraham's life. His name wasn't even Abraham, but Abram; meaning 'exalted father,' but he had no children. Abram was a 75-year-old man, but still living in his father's house. Think of how people, especially young men, are laughed at and scorned for living in their parents' homes today when they reach adulthood. Imagine a 75-year-old man man living in his father house! Though Abraham didn't have that much going on, he decided to change direction to alter his story. He obeyed the leading of the Lord by leaving his country and father's house, to go to the land the Lord promised to show him.

"Now the Lord had said to Abram:

"Get out of your country,
From your family
And from your father's house,
to a land that I will show you.
I will make you a great nation;
I will bless you
And make your name great;
And you shall be a blessing.
I will bless those who bless you,
And I will curse him who curses you;
And in you all the families of the earth shall be blessed."

- Genesis 12:1-3 NKJV

The key moment, however, is in verse 4.

ABRAHAM'S TURNING POINT

"So Abram departed as the Lord had spoken to him, and Lot went with him. And Abram was seventy-five years old when he departed from Haran."

So Abram departed... An action took place—Abram departed. He moved to inspire a move of God, which gave birth to the land and nation of Israel. Abraham left to lead!

He obeyed what God said. From that moment forward, he encountered so many moments that changed his life in one way or another—for the better not only for himself, but also for generations yet unborn. Abraham found favor in different ways wherever he went. He met great men who even ended up considering him more significant than them. Whenever opposition arose, God delivered him through it all. He became a friend of God, which was how he was able to reason with God about things—like saving Lot from Sodom and Gomorrah.

Abram and Sarai went through a name change. They became the Abraham and Sarah that we know today. Despite their old age, they became parents. Even after Sarah died, Abraham married again **and fathered several more children** (Genesis 25).

TURNING POINT: FROM ASHES TO BEAUTY

As easy as it sounds, his journey was not entirely that simple or neither was it all a cakewalk. During the process, there were times Abraham made some mistakes, just as every human being. He also exhibited a degree of weakness. The Lord told Abraham that he would have a child with his wife Sarah. The scripture says:

Then Abraham fell upon his face, and laughed, and said in his heart, Shall a child be born unto him that is a hundred years old? And shall Sarah, that is ninety years old, bear? And Abraham said unto God, O that Ishmael might live before thee!

- Genesis 17:17-18

Before this time, due to her fear of not being able to conceive, Sarah encouraged Abraham to have a child with Hagar, her handmaid. He did. Even though this happened, the Lord still granted what He promised Abraham. Sarah gave birth to a child at the age of 99.

Despite the failures of Abraham, God remained faithful to His promise in his life. Today, Abraham's turning point is still talked about. The legacy of his life and faith continue to inspire millions of people. We are encouraged to trust in God as much as he did.

*Look unto Abraham your father,
and unto Sarah that bare you:
for I called him alone, and blessed him,
and increased him.*

- Isaiah 51:2

Maybe you are feeling as if the things you had been hoping for, or the things God promised you do not seem to be coming. Do not lose hope. Hold on to your faith. Trust that the things God has spoken into your life will come to pass. Have faith and keep believing. Even when better options come, if God has not told you to take them, don't. Stay on the path of truth and faith.

That ye be not slothful, but followers of them who through faith and patience inherit the promises.

- Hebrews 6:12.

Your act of faith will never return void. Remember, a turning point is where the direction changes, taking you into a new part of the journey of your life. Different obstacles and situations may come, but as long as you retain your faith and confidence in God, all things will ultimately work for your good.

Trust in the Lord and lean not on your own understanding.

- Proverbs 3:5

Do not sit complacently when things are not going the right way in your life. Avoid complaining. Your words can be used for much more productive and powerful things.

What may appear as a delay or an obstacle is just a device of the enemy to discourage you. Keep on moving and do not retreat into hiding. Stay away from alternatives that seem to be better than the original plan God has given you. Those are also devices of the enemy designed to distract and divert you from where God is taking you.

Stretch your faith and dare to believe God just like Abraham did. Abraham stepped out. He wasn't aware of the full plan. He was just working on the instructions and promise God gave him. You do not need to know the entire plan before moving—or you may be waiting for ages!

ABRAHAM'S TURNING POINT

The Bible is full of assurances that God is with you, and that He will never leave you nor forsake you (Deut 13:6, Joshua 1:5, Hebrews 13:5). You have the Holy Spirit to guide you, to lead you and to assure you (John 14:26). So keep moving!

When Abraham decided to take that first step out of his father's house into the new direction God had for his life, a turning point began. I encourage you to emulate the faith of Abraham. Step out in faith; there is an entire legacy waiting to be yours.

Tassha Faison & Dr.Benard Etta with ministers friend in Demystifying Purpose conference Dallas, Texas 2014.

Chapter 3

JOSEPH'S TURNING POINT

*The Lord is with you,
always remember that.
And because He is with you,
nothing can bring you down.
No situation can keep you down.*

Sometimes our lives will consist of more than one defining moment—more than one turning point. Joseph's life shows us this possibility. He had several low moments, but every challenge he faced led to something more favorable and powerful.

Joseph was the son of Jacob and Rachel, and Jacob loved Joseph more than all his children because he was the son of his old age and he made him a coat of many colors (Genesis 37:3). As a result, the scripture says, his brothers hated him and could not speak peaceably to him.

On a certain day, when Jacob sent Joseph to his brothers, they stripped him of the beautiful robe his father gave him, and threw him into a pit. They ultimately sold him to Ishmaelite traders. In the

TURNING POINT: FROM ASHES TO BEAUTY

blink of an eye, Joseph went from being a beloved son in a wealthy household, to being a slave—sold by his own brothers.

Some people's lives take an unfortunate turn so suddenly, from betrayal, to losing a job, failing in school, or losing a loved one. It happens so fast that one is left wondering what on earth is going on. As Robert Schuller rightly said, "Tough times never last, but tough people do." Take note of this: through it all, Joseph's life did not end in despair.

Joseph was eventually sold as a slave to Potiphar, an officer of Pharaoh in Egypt. Even there, Joseph prospered. His master made Joseph the overseer of his house and all that he had, he put under his authority. God turn his pain to gain.

"The Lord was with Joseph, and he was a successful man; and he was in the house of his master the Egyptian. And his master saw that the Lord was with him and that the Lord made all he did to prosper in his hand. So Joseph found favor in his sight, and served him. Then he made him overseer of his house, and all that he had he put under his authority. So it was, from the time that he had made him overseer of his house and all that he had, that the Lord blessed the Egyptian's

house for Joseph's sake; and the blessing of the Lord was on all that he had in the house and in the field. Thus he left all that he had in Joseph's hand, and he did not know what he had except for the bread which he ate."

- Genesis 39:2-6

Even in Joseph's moment of darkness and a painful time of coming to terms with being betrayed by his brothers and serving as a slave, Joseph prospered because the Lord was with him. That is something worth noting. If you didn't know it, you better know it now. The Lord is with you right now. He is backing you up and able to turn your story into glory. He is ready to provide the increase in your efforts. Let this knowledge encourage and inspire you to keep moving in faith, knowing that God is working everything for your good (Rom 8:28).

Joseph's situation turned around for the better. He became an overseer in Potiphar's house. Potiphar entrusted Joseph with everything. From a slave to an overseer. That is grace. That is God!

Joseph encountered another moment that looked like a bad turn. Potiphar's wife tried to seduce him, but when he rejected her wish and ran away, Potiphar's wife framed him for rape. He was thrown into prison by his master, another bad turn and painful moment.

Maybe you have encountered that before. Just as everything was going well, suddenly something terrible happened, and you felt like you had gone 100 steps back. Imagine the progress Joseph made, and suddenly it was all gone in "the twinkling of an eye." The same master who trusted him with everything had him thrown into jail. Another bad turn that was not permanent. Look at this:

"So it was, when his master heard the words which his wife spoke to him, saying, "Your servant did to me after this manner," that his anger was aroused. Then Joseph's master took him and put him into the prison, a place where the king's prisoners were confined. And he was there in the prison. But the Lord was with Joseph and showed him mercy, and He gave him favor in the sight of the keeper of the prison. And the keeper of the prison committed to Joseph's hand all the prisoners who were in the prison; whatever they did there, it was his doing. The keeper of the prison did not look into anything that was under Joseph's

JOSEPH'S TURNING POINT

authority,[a] because the Lord was with him; and whatever he did, the Lord made it prosper."

- Genesis 39:19-23

In a place where only hopelessness and strife existed, Joseph prospered. God caused Joseph to find favor in the eyes of the prison keeper. He went from being a mere prisoner to a leader in jail.

Destiny can be delayed, but can't be denied. Joseph got entrusted with responsibility once again because the Lord was with Him. We all should be inspired to hold on to our hope and not to give up.

*"He sent a man before them,
even Joseph, who was sold for a servant: Whose feet they hurt with fetters: he was laid in iron: Until the time that his word came: the word of the LORD tried him. The king sent and loosed him; even the ruler of the people, and let him go free. He made him lord of his house, and ruler of all his substance: To bind his princes at his pleasure; and teach his senators wisdom."*

- Psalm 105:17-22

TURNING POINT: FROM ASHES TO BEAUTY

We all know how the drama unfolded. While serving the Lord in jail, the Lord used Joseph to interpret the dreams of his fellow prison inmates as recorded in Genesis 40 and 41. One of the inmates was freed and restored as Pharaoh's cup-bearer. During this period, the Lord gave Pharaoh a dream which the wise men of Egypt couldn't interpret and his cup-bearer told him how Joseph interpreted his dream while in prison and it came to pass. What looked like a crisis to Pharaoh became an opportunity to Joseph.

Joseph was called out of prison to stand before Pharaoh to interpret his dream. When he did, Joseph went from being a prisoner to becoming one of the key men in Pharaoh's administration. In fact, Pharaoh gave him charge over Egypt's economic affairs. That was a major turning point in his life. Under his guidance, Egypt was spared from the devastating effect of the seven years famine, which affected most of the world. At that time He reunited with his family and the rest of his days were peaceful and prosperous.

There are many things we can glean from the life of Joseph. He faced severe adversities, which were a result of other people's decisions, but everything still worked out for his good.

The turns in his life, which appeared to be horrible, ended up turning into platforms for him to flourish. They were not his end neither did they define him nor stop him. Listen! It can be the same for you.

If you are currently experiencing adverse circumstances as a result of what other people have done or are doing to you; or suddenly things just turned upside down—know that it isn't permanent. Take courage and take heart, knowing you are being positioned to flourish.

Do not let what you see stop or hinder you. Don't waste time complaining about how unfair everything is. Take control of the situation and take charge. You can only take charge by holding your peace, remaining confident and knowing that God is in control.

The Lord is with you always. Remember that nothing can bring you down. No situation can keep you down.

"What then shall we say to these things? If God is for us, who can be against us?"

- Romans 8:31

TURNING POINT: FROM ASHES TO BEAUTY

Pastor Tassha Faison, Apostle Elizabeth Hairston McBurrows and Apostle Bill Hamon

Chapter 4

MOSES' TURNING POINT

Do not let the things, which held you down before, to keep you down forever.

Moses is known as one of the greatest prophets of the Old Testament. He had a close relationship with God that was rare in those times—very rare. God used him mightily to deliver the Israelites from Egypt. He led them through the wilderness, bringing them close to the Promised Land before handing leadership over to his successor, Joshua. Even though Moses did not reach the Promised Land, he played a huge role in getting them out of Egypt, through the wilderness, and bringing them close to their inheritance.

Moses, however, did not start off like that. He wasn't always so close to and confident in God. Moses, a Hebrew baby, ended up being raised in the house of Pharaoh. After his mother put him in an ark made of bulrushes and set him on the river, the daughter of Pharaoh found him.

Moses had a prosperous life as a child in Pharaoh's house. Everything changed, however, the day he killed an Egyptian guard that was abusing a Hebrew slave. Moses then had to flee from Egypt. In a swift moment, Moses went from being a part of Pharaoh's household to being a fugitive as a result of his decision to murder someone.

Maybe you are where you are as a consequence of some of the decisions you have made. Don't worry. Don't be grieved. You'll find in this book that your past decisions do not have to define the rest of your future. Redemption is always possible.

Moses ended up in Midian and dwelled there for several years. Moses' turning point occurred while he was keeping the flock of Jethro (Exodus 3). Moses encountered a burning bush—a very well-known moment. That was where he met the Angel of the Lord.

"The Lord said, "I have in fact seen the affliction (suffering, desolation) of My people who are in Egypt, and have heard their cry because of their taskmasters (oppressors); for I know their pain and

MOSES' TURNING POINT

suffering. So I have come down to rescue them from the hand (power) of the Egyptians, and to bring them up from that land to a land [that is] good and spacious, to a land [b]flowing with milk and honey [a land of plenty]—to the place of the Canaanite, the Hittite, the Amorite, the Perizzite, the Hivite, and the Jebusite. Now, behold, the cry of the children of Israel has come to Me; and I have also seen how the Egyptians oppress them."

- Exodus 3:7-9

Moses was reluctant at first, and he asked God many questions, but later on he surrendered to the plan of God for his life. He agreed to what God had assigned him to do. Moses went from being a murderer to a deliverer of the Jews. That was the effect of his turning point.

Many other great things went on to happen through Moses. Many times, people let the mistakes they have made in their past to dominate the rest of their lives.

Even after repenting, people do not fully move on because of guilt and shame. Others are unable to be used of God by focusing on their weaknesses. Moses had a speech impediment. He was concerned that no one would take him seriously (Read Exodus 4). But God assured him of His presence and even gave Moses Aaron to speak on His behalf.

Your moment might not be a burning bush, but you have the Word of God to show you what God has called you to do. You know that God loves you, and He has great plans for you. While you may feel unqualified, realize this: if God could use a murderer who had a speech problem, what makes you think He cannot use you?

The same way God provided a solution for all of Moses' shortfalls and flaws, is the same way God has provided a solution to every single thing you think is hindering you from fulfilling the purpose He has for you.

Have you done things in your life that you are not happy about or seeing the effect of some of the bad decisions you have made? Even if you are still experiencing the repercussions, take note of this scripture. You have probably read it before. Read it again with understanding:

MOSES' TURNING POINT

"Therefore, if anyone is in Christ, he is a new creation; old things have passed away; behold, all things have become new."

- 2 Corinthians 5:17 NKJV

Whenever condemnation comes your way, always remind yourself that you are a new creation. Let your decisions today be different from those you made in the past. Let your motives be new. Do not let the things that held you down before to keep you down forever.

If you had a temper before, do not let it rule your mind. If you weren't very organized, let that change. That is what it means to be a new creation; a new mode of operation, a new way of thinking and a new way of handling things.

Moses may have been a murderer and a person who stuttered, but after his turning point, his identity changed. He became bold and wiser, functioning and speaking differently. The results he had were different.

His past became irrelevant. No one knew him as the murderer or the person who stuttered anymore. They soon knew him as the one whom God used to deliver the children of Israel out of Egypt and the one God used to give the Law to Israel. That was what happened when the life of Moses took an entirely different direction after his meeting with the Lord. If Moses could experience such a turnaround in his life, you can also believe God for your own.

> *By faith Moses, when he was born, was hid three months of his parents, because they saw he was a proper child; and they were not afraid of the king's commandment. By faith Moses, when he was come to years, refused to be called the son of Pharaoh's daughter; Choosing rather to suffer affliction with the people of God, than to enjoy the pleasures of sin for a season; Esteeming the reproach of Christ greater riches than the treasures in Egypt: for he had respect unto the recompense of the reward. By faith he forsook Egypt, not fearing the wrath of the king: for he endured, as seeing him who is invisible. Through faith he kept the Passover, and the sprinkling of blood, lest he that destroyed the firstborn should touch them. By faith they passed through the Red sea as by dry land: which the Egyptians assaying to do were drowned.*
>
> - Hebrews 11:23-29

Chapter 5

GIDEON'S TURNING POINT

*Let go of your insecurities.
Let go of your doubts.
Let go of your fears.
You need to move past them if you have any intention of achieving anything at all.*

But Gideon replied, "Sir, how can I save Israel? My family is the poorest in the whole tribe of Manasseh, and I am the least thought of in the entire family!"
- Judges 6:15 TLB

Gideon was at the bottom of the chain. Not only was his family the poorest in his entire tribe, but he was also the least in his family. That meant, no one paid him any serious attention. He wasn't very relevant to anyone.

Imagine that no one is thinking highly of you. Then suddenly, this strange figure comes and tells you that God is going to use you to deliver an entire nation. Some of you may be like that. You have been hurt by the people who were meant to be close to you. They have despised and abandoned you, leaving you insecure, and lacking confidence.

It may seem to you that you may not amount to much. You may have accepted that you are not destined to be the best in anything nor think anything great can come from you. Well, you need to realize this: The same Gideon, who said those words to the Angel of the Lord, about being the least in his family—and tribe—was the same person who ended up being used by God to deliver the Israelites—an entire nation—from the hand of the Midianites.

Gideon's turning point came at the moment the Angel of the Lord appeared to him. Though it took some time for Gideon to believe what the Angel of the Lord was saying, things took a different turn when he agreed to God's vision for his life and ran with the instruction given to him.

When the Lord confirmed his word to him via a sign as requested by Gideon, nothing could stand in his way any

GIDEON'S TURNING POINT

longer. He didn't allow his fears to get a hold of him; he did not stop moving.

> *"Jerubbaal (that is, Gideon—his other name) and his army got an early start and went as far as the spring of Harod. The armies of Midian were camped north of them, down in the valley beside the hill of Moreh."*
>
> - Judges 7:1

Have you ever asked yourself how this same timid Gideon was able to gather an army?

In the previous chapter, he spoke of coming from the least tribe and being the least in his family. But this same Gideon was able to mobilize an army within a short time. This was an army God even said was too big (Judges 7:2).

That is what happens when you agree to what God instructs, and you step out to do it. God's grace does not give you just what you need, but even more. God isn't just enough, He is too much.

David said, "My cup runs over." He can do exceeding, abundantly; above all we can ask or think. The same Gideon, who was not taken seriously before, became the man of the hour on whose leadership the destiny of his nation was resting. The same Gideon, who was timid and doubtful, became a person of authority, who led a charge to defeat the Midianites. His turning point arrived when he went from being timid to being brave. He transitioned from being the least to being a leader. He went from being at the bottom of the pile, to leading his nation to victory.

His story was possible because he chose not to let doubts and fears overwhelm him or stop him from doing God's bidding. The fact of the matter is, as you transition in your life, there will be moments when you feel afraid, doubtful, and inadequate. Just because you feel that way, doesn't mean you are as you think.

Keep on moving. When you make a decision to go after something, let that be your focus. When you decide to walk in line with something God has given you to do, He will stir up boldness in you to press forward. Don't allow your physical senses to limit you. Look inward and draw strength from the greater One in you.

Gideon's example should inspire you not to allow your background and what you think you don't have to define you.

GIDEON'S TURNING POINT

Gideon started by feeling inadequate, but look at the great assignment God had him fulfill!

Let go of your insecurities. Let go of your doubts. Let go of your fears. You need to move past them if you have any dream of achieving anything at all. These things are not a part of your identity. They are stumbling blocks designed to keep you from obtaining your goal.

Remember, Gideon didn't know what awaited him if he destroyed the altar of Baal, but when he did, the Lord raised his father Joash to defend him. God has a solution for every single challenge you are facing. He will send people to back you up. He will send people to assist you. He is God. What can He not do?

There are countless more examples of people in the Old Testament whose lives did an entire 360-degree shift: David, Elisha, Ruth, Esther, King Hezekiah, etc. There are also many examples in the New Testament—much more.

Chapter 6

NICODEMUS' TURNING POINT

Be receptive to those who walk in wisdom and speak life. They will impact your life positively.

"After dark one night a Jewish religious leader named Nicodemus, a member of the sect of the Pharisees, came for an interview with Jesus. "Sir," he said, "we all know that God has sent you to teach us. Your miracles are proof enough of this."

Jesus replied, "With all the earnestness I possess I tell you this: Unless you are born again, you can never get into the Kingdom of God."

"Born again!"exclaimed Nicodemus. "What do you mean? How can an old man go back into his mother's womb and be born again?"

TURNING POINT: FROM ASHES TO BEAUTY

Jesus replied, "What I am telling you so earnestly is this: Unless one is born of water and the Spirit, he cannot enter the Kingdom of God.

Men can only reproduce human life, but the Holy Spirit gives new life from heaven; so don't be surprised at my statement that you must be born again! 8ust as you can hear the wind but can't tell where it comes from or where it will go next, so it is with the Spirit. We do not know on whom he will next bestow this life from heaven."

"What do you mean?" Nicodemus asked.

Jesus replied, "You, a respected Jewish teacher, and yet you don't understand these things? I am telling you what I know and have seen—and yet you won't believe me. But if you don't even believe me when I tell you about such things as these that happen here among men, how can you possibly believe if I tell you what is going on in heaven?"
- John 3:1-12

Nicodemus was a well-respected religious leader—a Pharisee. The Pharisees were

NICODEMUS' TURNING POINT

known for trying to disrupt and frustrate Jesus' ministry. They refused to believe that He was the Messiah. They often tried to debate with Jesus and ask Him screwball questions, but their plots were never successful.

Nicodemus experienced a different kind of turning point. He received a total shift in his religious thinking. What he thought he had known all along was proven wrong in one conversation with Christ. He received the Truth through one encounter that challenged his theology. Nicodemus could not wrap his head around the whole concept of being "born again." When he asked Jesus about what it meant, Jesus went on to explain what being born again was about.

Nicodemus had to let go of his former thoughts. He discovered the truth, and it looked nothing like what he had been teaching and believing beforehand. A turning point in his belief system led him to become a fan of Jesus Christ. He left behind his former life of religion and condemnation and sought to know more about the Way, the Truth and the Life (Jesus Christ).

Nicodemus saith unto them, (he that came to Jesus by night, being one of them

TURNING POINT: FROM ASHES TO BEAUTY

- John 7:50

Turning points arrive in diverse ways. They happen to people differently. Maybe some of you can relate to how you left behind a former life to embrace the newness in Jesus Christ. Maybe there was a belief, something you had been holding on to for so long which turned out to be false. You exchanged it for the truth.

It isn't really about how the turning point comes or happens. What happens afterward is what matters. Your turning point could occur in the form of a simple conversation, but the impact it will leave on your life is colossal. That is why; being receptive to those who walk in wisdom and speak life is important. They will impact your life positively.

Chapter 7

THE WOMAN AT THE WELL

Everything from the past won't matter. What you do from the present onwards is what will count.

"Soon a Samaritan woman came to draw water, and Jesus asked her for a drink. He was alone at the time as his disciples had gone into the village to buy some food. The woman was surprised that a Jew would ask a "despised Samaritan" for anything—usually they wouldn't even speak to them!—and she remarked about this to Jesus.

He replied, "If you only knew what a wonderful gift God has for you, and who I am, you would ask me for some living water!"

"But you don't have a rope or a bucket," she said, "and this is a very deep well! Where would you get this living water? And besides, are you greater than our ancestor Jacob? How can you offer better

TURNING POINT: FROM ASHES TO BEAUTY

water than this which he and his sons and cattle enjoyed?"

Jesus replied that people soon became thirsty again after drinking this water. "But the water I give them," he said, "becomes a perpetual spring within them, watering them forever with eternal life."

"Please, sir," the woman said, "give me some of that water! Then I'll never be thirsty again and won't have to make this long trip out here every day."

"Go and get your husband," Jesus told her.

"But I'm not married," the woman replied.

"All too true!" Jesus said. "For you have had five husbands, and you aren't even married to the man you're living with now."

"Sir," the woman said, "you must be a prophet. But say, tell me, why is it that you Jews insist that Jerusalem is the only place of worship, while we Samaritans claim it is here at Mount Gerizim, where our ancestors worshiped?"

THE WOMAN AT THE WELL

Jesus replied, "The time is coming, ma'am, when we will no longer be concerned about whether to worship the Father here or in Jerusalem. For it's not where we worship that counts, but how we worship—is our worship spiritual and real? Do we have the Holy Spirit's help? For God is Spirit, and we must have his help to worship as we should. The Father wants this kind of worship from us. But you Samaritans know so little about him, worshiping blindly, while we Jews know all about him, for salvation comes to the world through the Jews."

The woman said, "Well, at least I know that the Messiah will come—the one they call Christ—and when he does, he will explain everything to us."

Then Jesus told her, "I am the Messiah!"

Just then his disciples arrived. They were surprised to find him talking to a woman, but none of them asked him why, or what they had been discussing.

Then the woman left her waterpot beside the well and went back to the village and told everyone,

TURNING POINT: FROM ASHES TO BEAUTY

"Come and meet a man who told me everything I ever did! Can this be the Messiah?"

- John 4:7-29

The Samaritan woman, who encountered Jesus at the well, experienced a turning point that shifted her reasoning, her way of thinking, and even her identity. The scripture depicts the conversation Jesus had with her. Samaritans and Jews did not see eye to eye. That issue passed by swiftly once Jesus reached out to her. Initially, she thought that He was just a prophet speaking of the Messiah.

Her view shifted when she realized that she could be talking to the Messiah himself. Once she caught the revelation, she ran with it and went to announce it to the people in her community. In a very short space of time, the woman went from being a Samaritan woman (with serious relationship issues) to being a messenger for the Messiah. Her report led to many people from the Samaritan village coming to hear what Christ had to say.

That is what happens when your life experiences a turnaround. When you hit a turning point, and agree to move in that new direction, the ripple effect that occurs has the potential to be huge. Your actions would start to affect those around you positively, and you will start channeling life to those around you. You lead them to the Light. Everything from the past won't matter anymore. What you do from the present onward is what will count.

Minister Tassha Faison with friends.

Chapter 8

THE ADULTEROUS WOMAN

God can turn your mess into a message and your trash into treasure.

Jesus returned to the Mount of Olives, but early the next morning he was back again at the Temple. A crowd soon gathered, and he sat down and talked to them. As he was speaking, the Jewish leaders and Pharisees brought a woman caught in adultery and placed her out in front of the staring crowd.

"Teacher," they said to Jesus, "this woman was caught in the very act of adultery. Moses' law says to kill her. What about it?"

They were trying to trap him into saying something they could use against him, but Jesus stooped down and wrote in the dust with his finger. 7 They kept demanding an answer, so he stood up again and said, "All right, hurl the stones at her until she

TURNING POINT: FROM ASHES TO BEAUTY

dies. But only he who never sinned may throw the first!"

Then he stooped down again and wrote some more in the dust. 9 And the Jewish leaders slipped away one by one, beginning with the eldest, until only Jesus was left in front of the crowd with the woman.

Then Jesus stood up again and said to her, "Where are your accusers? Didn't even one of them condemn you?"

"No, sir," she said.

And Jesus said, "Neither do I. Go and sin no more."

- John 8:1-11 TLB

The case of the adulterous woman, whom the Pharisees and Jewish leaders wished to have stoned, is a more public and a dramatic example of a turning point in one's life. She got caught in the act of adultery and by law, she should have been stoned. That was what the people were about doing, but Jesus showed her

THE ADULTEROUS WOMAN

mercy and rescued her from her potential peril.

Jesus challenged the crowd who was so ready to have her stoned by simply stating that whoever is without sin, be the first to cast the stone. Upon realizing that none of them were as white as snow, they all left. Jesus saved the woman and that initiated a turning point in her life.

Jesus turned her from condemnation to freedom by telling her to go and sin no more. He was more interested in seeing her live a life free from sin than He was interested in whatever she been caught in, as he stated that he would not condemn her. She was free.

That was her turning point, and that is a turning point for many people today. Individuals who have come from tainted backgrounds filled with mistakes and bad decisions can experience forgiveness. Your sins can be blotted out (Isaiah 43:25). That is the greatest turning point—going from being a sinner to becoming saved and brought into a life of liberty; a life free from the sting and oppression that comes from sin. A life filled with grace and a life filled with love.

A life that gives you total access to what the Father has set aside for you. The outcome is so much bigger than it sounds. To be free from sin means that you are free from guilt and death. New decisions. Better decisions. Everything about you points towards channeling life and being light.

The adulterous woman was also set free from a religious system that wanted her death for her sin. Mercy set her free from "jungle justice." She received hope when not too long before, her situation appeared hopeless. She was delivered from death and set free from judgment and given another chance.

I'm sure that her moment was eternally unforgettable. In the midst of people calling for bloodshed, there was One who wanted her set free. There was One who loved her and desired to see her living a higher life. There was someone who was ready to defend her, even though she did not deserve it. Jesus openly dealt with those who were quick to judge. It is moments like that when love is demonstrated that results in a turnaround in people's lives.

A friend of mine once told me why she returned to Christ after backsliding. She said it was the love God showed her that drew her back. Love covered her even when she tried to reject it. Love reached out to her time and time again. That was

THE ADULTEROUS WOMAN

her turning point, and ever since then, her life has gone higher and higher. That is the power of God's love. And it is readily available to turn your life around as well.

Chapter 9

THE TWELVE APOSTLES

Your life can change too, the same way the disciples' lives changed. All that is required is for you to keep moving in your relationship with Jesus.

"Jesus called his twelve disciples to him and gave them authority to cast out evil spirits and to heal every kind of sickness and disease.

Here are the names of his twelve disciples: Simon (also called Peter), Andrew (Peter's brother), James (Zebedee's son), John (James's brother), Philip, Bartholomew, Thomas, Matthew (the tax collector), James (Alphaeus's son), Thaddaeus, Simon (a member of "The Zealots," a subversive political party), Judas Iscariot (the one who betrayed him).

Jesus sent them out with these instructions: "Don't go to the Gentiles or the Samaritans, but only to the people of

TURNING POINT: FROM ASHES TO BEAUTY

Israel—God's lost sheep. Go and announce to them that the Kingdom of Heaven is near.

Heal the sick, raise the dead,

cure the lepers, and cast out demons. Give as freely as you have received!"
- Matthew 10:1-8

The twelve Apostles are men of God still spoken of today as Pioneers of faith who ignited the flame of the message of Christ to the nations. Their mark on the world is being talked about to this very day. They were men on fire for the Gospel. To them, it wasn't something they just believed in; they identified with the Gospel. It became a part of their life. It was something they experienced and the Truth they were willing to die for to defend.

They did not preach a blind message as many do today. They saw Christ and walked with him. They were witnesses to His life, death, resurrection and ascension to heaven.

With the power of the Holy Spirit in them, they performed mighty miracles and went everywhere preaching. They reached out to millions of people. They were utterly and completely sold out to spreading the message of Christ.

They experience great persecution. Most of them went through inhumane forms of death, but none of the darkness that tried to overcome them could hinder them. They continued spreading the good news of the Kingdom of God until death.

Mighty men of God they were, but they did not start off like that. They asked questions time and time again, which Jesus expected them to know better. They bickered amongst each other and weren't the most morally upright people when Jesus first met them. They did not understand most of the things Jesus taught. They did not trust Jesus all the time. At one point they couldn't even cast out demons (Matthew 14:17-20).

When Jesus was arrested and crucified, they abandoned him—except for John, who remained during the crucifixion. Even Peter, one of the men at the forefront of the apostles denied Christ three times. Thomas doubted the news of Jesus' resurrection until Jesus appeared to the disciples at another occasion and showed him the nail marks in His hands. The disciples were not perfect, but their walk with Christ and being under His leadership made them a force for the Gospel that could not be silenced. They were arrested and jailed, but most of the time, the Lord intervened like when Peter was taken out of prison by an angel (Acts 12:5-17). Being beaten and persecuted never stopped their mission.

They spoke the Gospel publicly, and reached out to whomever they could. They carried the presence of God so profoundly, and supernatural miracles took place wherever they went. People would lay the sick on beds and mats across the street in hopes of Peter's shadow passing over them for their healing (Acts 5:15). The Apostles carried the character and nature of Christ in them so much that it became a part of them and manifested in the natural.

The disciples were an odd combination of men from different backgrounds, who were linked by one—Jesus Christ. Though they came from contrasting backgrounds, they all had one common turning point. Their passion for Jesus Christ and His message united them. Even after they had received the Holy Ghost, they made mistakes here and there (e.g. when Peter forsook the Gentiles whenever Jews were around

(Galatians 2:11-21). The move of God through them was immense.

Christ changed timid and inadequate disciples, and they partook in his glory. That is the power of having an encounter with Jesus. No part of you remains the same. Through fellowship with Christ, study of the Word and communication with Him, you become more and more like Him. The new creation in you begins to manifest in the natural.

An encounter with Christ is one of the most important turning points. From there, everything starts changing. It is where you have access to everything and begins a remarkable journey similar to that of the disciples. More of this will be discussed in the next chapter when I speak of Paul.

Just know this, your life can change in the same way the disciples lives changed. All that is required is for you to come to Christ and dedicate your life to walk with Him. If you are already a believer, keep moving in your relationship with Jesus Christ. Holding on to him and focusing on Him as you run your race.

TURNING POINT: FROM ASHES TO BEAUTY

"Therefore we also, since we are surrounded by so great a cloud of witnesses, let us lay aside every weight, and the sin which so easily ensnares us, and let us run with endurance the race that is set before us, looking unto Jesus, the author and finisher of our faith, who for the joy that was set before Him endured the cross, despising the shame, and has sat down at the right hand of the throne of God."

- Hebrews 12:1-2

Minister Tassha Faison &
Apostle Carlos White

Chapter 10

PAUL'S TURNING POINT

So, be encouraged and know that nothing truly is impossible.

The Apostle Paul was another man who was used mightily by God. His writings are what make up the majority of the epistles of the New Testament. He was not a part of the Twelve Apostles, but God used him just as effectively. Some argue he was used even more than the other Apostles.

Paul's primary ministry focus was more towards reaching the Gentiles. He had a deep love for people and he, like the Twelve, was sold out for the Gospel. He was also determined to see the Gospel spread and the church grow.

His letters to the believers in different locations consisted of exhortations, deep teachings, corrections, and admonishments. Paul was passionate about seeing as many people as possible living the higher life God had called them to live.

He endured great persecution—even from believers. There were times he had disagreements with believers who were struggling with the Law and failing to walk in Grace. He had a couple of arguments with people he walked with, e.g. Barnabas.

Miraculous demonstrations happened through this man. He spoke publicly, and even when he got arrested and was due to face trial, he never ceased. He continued to preach and teach. He was unapologetic about his life in Christ; He embraced it totally. He rejoiced in his persecution and trials.

"For I consider that the sufferings of this present time are not worthy to be compared with the glory which shall be revealed in us."

- Romans 8:18 NKJV

"And not only that, but we also glory in tribulations, knowing that tribulation produces perseverance; and perseverance, character; and character, hope. Now hope does not disappoint, because the love of God has been poured out in our hearts by the Holy Spirit who was given to us."

- Romans 5:3-10

PAUL'S TURNING POINT

Paul wasn't always a saint. His name wasn't even Paul before he encountered Christ. He was known as Saul of Tarsus. In fact, before his turning point, Paul used to be one of the leading individuals in charge of persecuting and murdering believers, or anyone who claimed to preach the Gospel. His encounter with Christ on his way to Damascus would transform his life forever.

"Then Saul, still breathing threats and murder against the disciples of the Lord, went to the high priest and asked letters from him to the synagogues of Damascus, so that if he found any who were of the Way, whether men or women, he might bring them bound to Jerusalem.

As he journeyed he came near Damascus, and suddenly a light shone around him from heaven. Then he fell to the ground, and heard a voice saying to him, "Saul, Saul, why are you persecuting Me?"

And he said, "Who are You, Lord?" Then the Lord said, "I am Jesus, whom you are persecuting. It is hard for you to kick against the goads."

TURNING POINT: FROM ASHES TO BEAUTY

So he, trembling and astonished, said, "Lord, what do You want me to do?"

Then the Lord said to him, "Arise and go into the city, and you will be told what you must do."

And the men who journeyed with him stood speechless, hearing a voice but seeing no one. Then Saul arose from the ground, and when his eyes were opened he saw no one. But they led him by the hand and brought him into Damascus. And he was three days without sight, and neither ate nor drank."

- Acts 9:1-9 NKJV

From there, Paul was anointed by Ananias and he received his sight. He remained in Damascus for a few more days before proceeding to the work God had assigned him.

Paul's turning point began when he had a remarkable encounter with God that left a physical imprint on him and an eternal one in his heart. It was this experience that gave him a boldness many had not seen before. It was what gave him assurance. It was what gave him peace—especially in times of trials

PAUL'S TURNING POINT

and tribulations. It took a while for believers to trust him—considering his past. Once they saw that he was genuinely converted, they opened up to him.

The moment Paul moved on from his turning point and walked in his new direction, things of immense magnitude started happening. Like the Twelve Apostles, the works God did through Paul are still spoken of and even seen to this day.

Considering Paul's past, this was truly miraculous. The persecutor soon became the persecuted. Be encouraged and know that nothing is truly impossible. There is nothing that can separate you from God's love and what He wants to do through you.

"For I am persuaded that neither death nor life, nor angels nor principalities nor powers, nor things present nor things to come, nor height nor depth, nor any other created thing, shall be able to separate us from the love of God which is in Christ Jesus our Lord."
- Romans 8:38

Paul wrote the above text. If a man who used to kill believers—God's children

—could confidently hold on to his new life and the vision of the Gospel, how much more you?

Chapter 11

MY STORY & MY TURNING POINT

Push yourself until that discipline goes from being a challenge to being a habit. Push yourself until you see growth and significance in your life.

I was a very smart kid throughout school. I received academic scholarships to college, but I had a big problem. I lacked discipline. I was a spoiled brat who thought I knew it all. Once I went off to college, far away from home, my life changed—for the worse.

My life became much, much worse. I experienced things that were very hard to imagine—painful things. Things got so bad that I almost lost my mind. I slipped into a very dark place. I lost all hope.

I got to a point where all I wanted to do was take my own life. I thought that suicide was the answer. But something inside me was also desperately hoping for a change. Despite the darkness I was immersed in, there was something in me crying out for light; something better than suicide.

I remember talking to myself at that moment. I said, "Something has to change now, or I am going to kill myself." Little did I know, that was the beginning of my turning point.

An Army recruiter heard me—how, I have no idea—but she came over and prayed for me. Not only did she do that, she also offered me an opportunity to serve in the United States Army.

I decided to join the army, even though I was still a mess. I was still struggling with discipline. But this was different. I was in an environment that was not going to let me have my way. My mindset underwent an intense makeover. I learned, unlearned and relearned in a very short time period.

I learned discipline the hard way. It was either do things the army way, or experience worse. Through daily repeated training, my mindset began to yield to the change. I formed new habits.

Self-discipline became a part of me. I started to embrace it and walk in it. The more I did, the easier it became. I began growing, and I started to become successful. That is when I realized that it takes discipline to experience change and stick to it. It takes discipline to have a made up mind. Physical discipline is necessary, but spiritual discipline is more important.

The beginning of change was hard—very hard. With the assistance of drill sergeants always pushing me past my limits, I made it.

This is what I wish to do for you. This is why I wrote this book. As a life coach, I genuinely want to push you beyond your limitations. Go beyond any self-pity you may be holding inside. Break past the hindrances that have been keeping you behind.

You need discipline to stay on the road of change. You need discipline even after your turning point. Otherwise, you will end up slipping into habits of the old—or worse. Push yourself until that discipline goes from being a challenge to being a habit. Push yourself until you see growth and significance in your life.

Refer to this book anytime you feel like giving up. Remember how many before you were able to continue on the path of change against all odds. Once you master one level of discipline, keep moving up. Gain more knowledge and master the next level. It is a process that requires a considerable amount of focus. It is like

Hebrews 12:1-2 says, we are to keep our eyes on Jesus as we run this race.

Jesus never lost focus, no matter what distractions came His way. His relationship with the Father grew constantly. He never neglected the things He was meant to do.

Chapter 12

REFLECTION SCRIPTURES AND HELPFUL QUOTES

No Pain, No Gain...

For those who are out of shape physically, to begin training requires enduring significant pain. The journey of fitness is not easy initially, but over time it becomes a part of you. It even becomes a source of enjoyment and pleasure—especially when you see the results.

Disciplined training leads to physical agility, strength, and health. Those in shape physically are more likely to take part in, excel at, and truly enjoy physical activities. By comparison, spiritual fitness is even more important.

But reject profane and old wives' fables, and exercise yourself toward godliness. For bodily exercise profits a little, but godliness is profitable for all things, having promise of the life that now is and of that which is to come.

TURNING POINT: FROM ASHES TO BEAUTY

- 1 Timothy 4:7-8 NJKV

"Do you not know that in a race all the runners run, but only one receives the prize? So run that you may obtain it. Run in the same way with determination to win."

- 1 Corinthians 9:24 NKJV

The disciples must be led by the Spirit "For as many as are led by the Spirit of God, these are sons of God."

- Romans 8:14

Oswald Chambers: "The Sermon on the Mount is not a set of principles to be obeyed apart from identification with Jesus Christ. The Sermon on the Mount is a statement of the life we will live when the Holy Spirit is getting his way with us."

For God did not give us a spirit of timidity, but a spirit of power, of love and of self-discipline.

- 2 Tim 1:7 (NIV)

REFLECTION SCRIPTURES

But the fruit of the Spirit is love, joy, peace, patience, kindness, goodness, faithfulness, gentleness and self-control... Since we live by the Spirit, let us keep in step with the Spirit.

- Gal 5:22-23,25 (NIV)

"..that each of you should know how to possess his own vessel in sanctification and honor,

not in passion of lust, like the Gentiles who do not know God;

that no one should take advantage of and defraud his brother in this matter, because the Lord is the avenger of all such, as we also forewarned you and testified.

For God did not call us to uncleanness, but in holiness.

Therefore he who rejects this does not reject man, but God, who has also given[a] us His Holy Spirit."

- 1 Thessalonians 4:4-8

Practice What You Are Not Good At...

Dallas Willard said, "People who think that they are spiritually superior because they make a practice of a discipline such as fasting are entirely missing the point. The need for the extensive practice of a given discipline is an indication of our weakness, not our strength. As a rule of thumb: if it is easy for us to engage in a certain discipline, we probably don't need to practice it. The disciplines we need to practice are precisely the ones we are not 'good at' and hence do not enjoy."

* * *

These are just scriptures and helpful quotes that will encourage you as you achieve and maintain your discipline. It is one of the major things needed to remain on the correct path leading to your turning point. Remember that it is never too late for change. God is capable of changing anyone—no matter how impossible they may seem.

Be encouraged. You are destined for greatness. There are particular things that are required to get you there and to

REFLECTION SCRIPTURES

keep you on the road there. It is definitely well with you.

You will reach your turning point. Any time you feel like giving up, pick up this book, go through it and remember that God will give you everything that it takes to keep you moving forward.

WHAT IS YOUR TURNING POINT?

WHAT IS YOUR TURNING POINT?

_____

_____

_____

_____

_____

_____

_____

_____

_____

_____

_____

WHAT IS YOUR TURNING POINT?

WHAT IS YOUR TURNING POINT?

_____

_____

_____

_____

_____

_____

_____

_____

_____

_____

MY ACTION STEPS

MY ACTION STEPS

_____

_____

_____

_____

_____

_____

_____

_____

_____

_____

MY ACTION STEPS

_____

_____

_____

_____

_____

_____

_____

_____

_____

_____

_____

MY ACTION STEPS

_____

_____

_____

_____

_____

_____

_____

_____

_____

_____

ABOUT THE AUTHOR

Pastor Tassha Faison
Turning Point Life Coaching, LLC

Pastor Tassha Faison is the founder and CEO of United and Spiritually Armed Forces, Inc (2012) and Turning Point LLC, which was established in 2016 to help individuals, groups and entrepreneurs attain their goals.

She is also the Regional Director of Women with A Call International (WWACI) and President of a local WWACI Branch in Fort Hood, Texas under the Leadership of its Founder, Dr. Elizabeth Hairston-McBurrows.

Tassha received several leadership awards while serving in the army. Though retired, Tassha remains a great asset to the soldiers who are still serving.

She has a heart for the Kingdom of God and her local community. Despite several turning points in her life, she has embraced the mandate always to impact lives in a positive manner.

Her passion is helping others shape their lives physically, mentally and mostly spiritually because she comprehends that listening to God is essential for a successful life's journey.

A great motivator and purpose-driven minister of the gospel, Pastor Faison believes in empowering the whole man and not focusing on weakness.

Tassha earned a Bachelor of Science in Human Services and later went on to obtain a Masters of Divinity with an emphasis in chaplaincy services. She is a graduate of The Apostolic/Prophetic Connection's, Inc (TAPC) under the leadership of Apostle Elizabeth Hairston-McBurrows.

Pastor Faison is the mother of two sons who are progressively pursuing their education and functioning as outstanding athletes in the community. She serves as administrative assistant for Apostle Elizabeth Hairston–McBurrows. She is also an entrepreneur, Author, mentor and a certified life coach with the John Maxwell Team.

www.ingramcontent.com/pod-product-compliance
Lightning Source LLC
Chambersburg PA
CBHW071315110426
42743CB00042B/2431